# The SECRET GARDENS

### of FRANCES HODGSON BURNETT

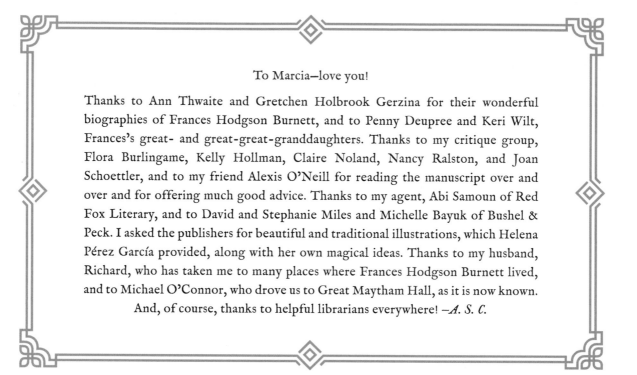

To Marcia—love you!

Thanks to Ann Thwaite and Gretchen Holbrook Gerzina for their wonderful biographies of Frances Hodgson Burnett, and to Penny Deupree and Keri Wilt, Frances's great- and great-great-granddaughters. Thanks to my critique group, Flora Burlingame, Kelly Hollman, Claire Noland, Nancy Ralston, and Joan Schoettler, and to my friend Alexis O'Neill for reading the manuscript over and over and for offering much good advice. Thanks to my agent, Abi Samoun of Red Fox Literary, and to David and Stephanie Miles and Michelle Bayuk of Bushel & Peck. I asked the publishers for beautiful and traditional illustrations, which Helena Pérez García provided, along with her own magical ideas. Thanks to my husband, Richard, who has taken me to many places where Frances Hodgson Burnett lived, and to Michael O'Connor, who drove us to Great Maytham Hall, as it is now known. And, of course, thanks to helpful librarians everywhere! —A. S. C.

Text copyright © 2024 by Angelica Shirley Carpenter

Illustrations copyright © 2024 by Helena Pérez García

Published by Bushel & Peck Books, a family-run publishing house in Fresno, California, that believes in uplifting children with the highest standards of art, music, literature, and ideas. Find beautiful books for gifted young minds at www.bushelandpeckbooks.com.

Type set in Jacob Riley, Calder Script, and Calder Dark.

Photograph of Frances Hodgson Burnett sourced from US Library of Congress, 2002697460.

Bushel & Peck Books is dedicated to fighting illiteracy all over the world. For every book we sell, we donate one to a child in need—book for book. To nominate a school or an organization to receive free books, please visit www.bushelandpeckbooks.com.

LCCN: 2024931580

ISBN: 978-1-63819-150-6

First Edition

Printed in China

1 3 5 7 9 10 8 6 4 2

# The SECRET GARDENS

of

## FRANCES HODGSON BURNETT

ANGELICA
SHIRLEY CARPENTER

Illustrated by
HELENA PÉREZ GARCÍA

BUSHEL
& PECK
BOOKS

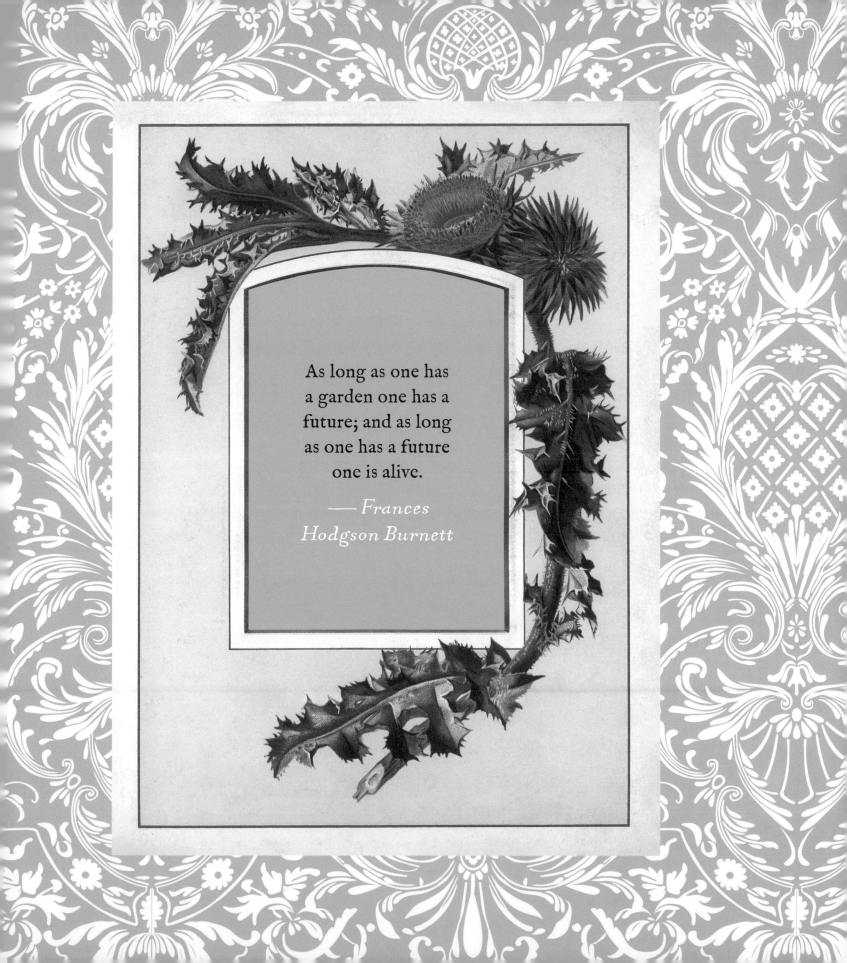

As long as one has
a garden one has a
future; and as long
as one has a future
one is alive.

—— *Frances
Hodgson Burnett*

anny Hodgson lived in an ordinary house in an ordinary English village. The inside was ordinary. The sofa and chairs and nursery were ordinary.

But Fanny Hodgson *wasn't* ordinary.

With a *blink* of her eye, fairies filled the rosebushes.

With the *wave* of her hand, elephants and tigers prowled the lilacs.

From under the apple tree, clouds became *moving* maps of islands and mountains.

Fanny could imagine

*anything.*

It was a good thing, too. **"We're moving to the city,"**
Mamma said one day.

Fanny stared. How could they leave her garden? But
Mamma knew best. She was a widow with five children
to support. She worked hard, running her late husband's
store in Manchester, England.

At their new home, closer to the store, Fanny watched entire families—even children—trudging through the dark, early morning streets to work in the mills. The houses were gray. The smoky air was gray. Life was gray.

But Fanny?
She could imagine

*anything.*

Nearby stood a high brick wall with a mysterious green door. What was behind it? Fanny's mind buzzed with curiosity, but the door was always locked.

Then one day, as if by magic,

*it opened.*

Inside was a walled garden, filled with rubbish and ugly weeds that *pricked* her fingers. Not for long. "You are *roses*," Fanny said. "You are *violets* and *lilies* and *daffodils*." Soon beautiful trees arched overhead, and carpets of fragrant flowers spread beneath her feet. The old garden *bloomed* that day in her imagination.

But as years passed, life got harder. Manchester businesses failed. Fanny had to drop out of school—her mother could no longer afford the fees. When Mamma was forced to sell the store, Fanny knew their money could not last.

Then an uncle wrote from America. If they moved near him, he said, he could find work for the boys.

After two weeks crossing the stormy Atlantic and days on the bumpy train, the Hodgsons reached their new home—a log cabin in a small village in Tennessee. Unfortunately, the boys couldn't earn as much money as they hoped. Sometimes the family went hungry.

But Fanny? She could imagine *anything.*

There were no jobs for girls, so fifteen-year-old Fanny
*invented* one, starting the town's first school. Eight students
paid their fees with cabbages, eggs, and potatoes. She read them
Shakespeare, and they teased her about her British accent.

All the while, Fanny's mind whirled with stories. *Sassafras, sumac, dogwood* —Tennessee plants had magical names. In the woods behind her house, Fanny built a secret room, weaving walls from branches and vines.

There she *dreamed* up story after story. If only she could rewrite her own family's story. Maybe she could! Fanny could imagine *anything*.

Magazines, like those she borrowed from
neighbors, *paid* for stories. Might one buy hers?
But she had no money for paper, envelopes, or stamps.
Then her sisters told her that neighbor girls had earned a
dollar selling wild grapes at the market. The next week, five girls
picked together and soon Fanny had money for supplies. Carefully,
she wrote out a love story and sent it to a magazine.

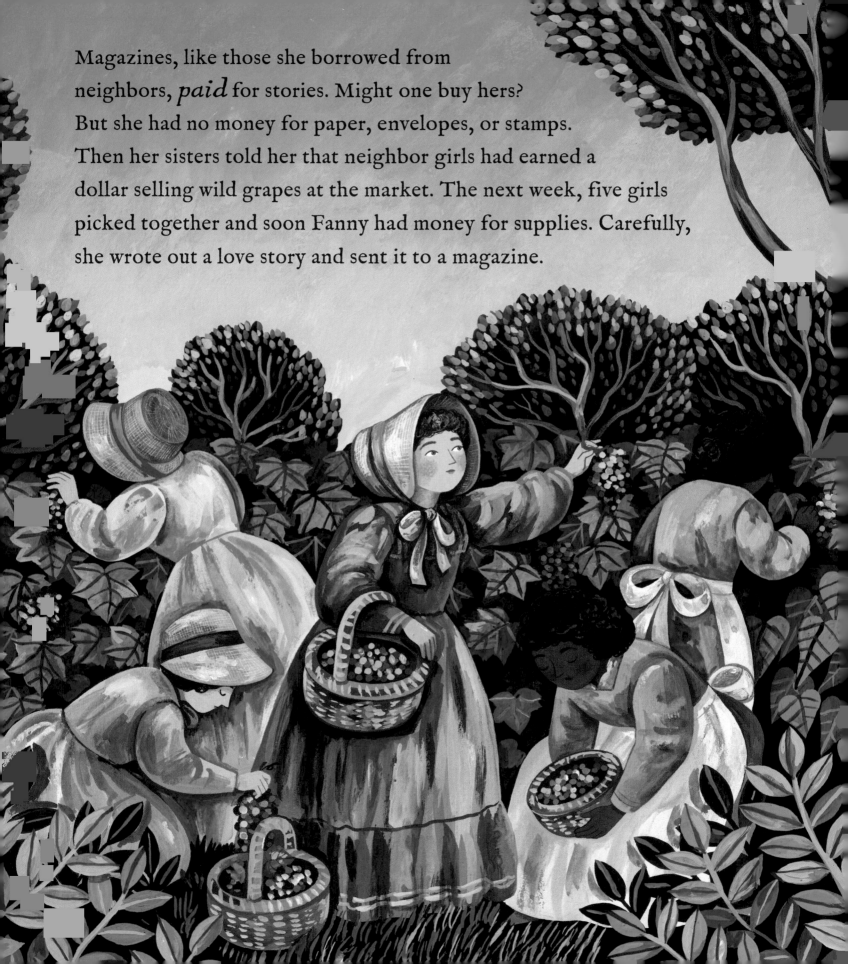

One day, a letter came with a check for thirty-five dollars—enough to feed the family for weeks! The magazine had bought her story and, best of all, the editor wanted *more*.

By the time she was nineteen, Fanny had sold enough stories to move her family to a larger house in Knoxville.

Five years later, she married a young eye doctor named Swan Burnett and they had two sons, Lionel and Vivian. The new family settled in Washington, DC. Swan didn't earn much at first, but Fanny knew what to do. She supported them all by writing novels for adults. Then, dropping her nickname, she reinvented herself as the author Frances Hodgson Burnett.

Her sons missed her when she wrote all day. "Why don't you write some stories that little boys would like to read?" Vivian asked. So she wrote *Little Lord Fauntleroy*, a book about an American boy who goes to England to live with his *grumpy* grandfather. She ended the story with a *fancy* garden party.

The book became an international *bestseller!*
Soon Frances could afford to take her sons to Italy,
Paris, and London. Wherever their steamship docked,
reporters greeted the famous author.

But money couldn't buy happiness. Tragedy struck when fifteen-year-old Lionel fell ill with tuberculosis. In those days, there was no cure. After months of sickness, Lionel died in his mother's arms. Frances thought her heart would *break*. She never got over her loss, but *love* for Vivian kept her going, even through a divorce.

Eight years later, Frances rented Maytham Hall, a country estate in the South of England. Behind the house stood a walled garden. Inside, she could hardly walk through the *tangled* weeds that covered everything, even the trees.

But Frances could imagine *anything*—and this time, she would make it real.

She spent her happiest spring ever, pruning, weeding, and digging in the damp earth. The gardener helped her plant bulbs, borders, and three hundred rosebushes. And by August, her first, very own garden . . .

. . . looked just the way she'd *imagined* it.

Frances's garden became her outdoor study. A friendly robin kept her company there while she wrote *A Little Princess*, a story about a girl who uses her imagination, like Frances, to forget her troubles.

Frances herself *never* forgot what it was like to suffer hardship. She gave money to the needy and shared Maytham with local villagers, inviting them to garden parties like the one in *Little Lord Fauntleroy*.

fter ten years, Maytham Hall felt like her own, but, sad to say, it was not. Her perfect world *shattered* when the owner decided to sell. Frances could not afford to buy it, but giving it up felt like losing a dear family member. On her last, grieving visit to the garden, the robin appeared, seeming to say goodbye.

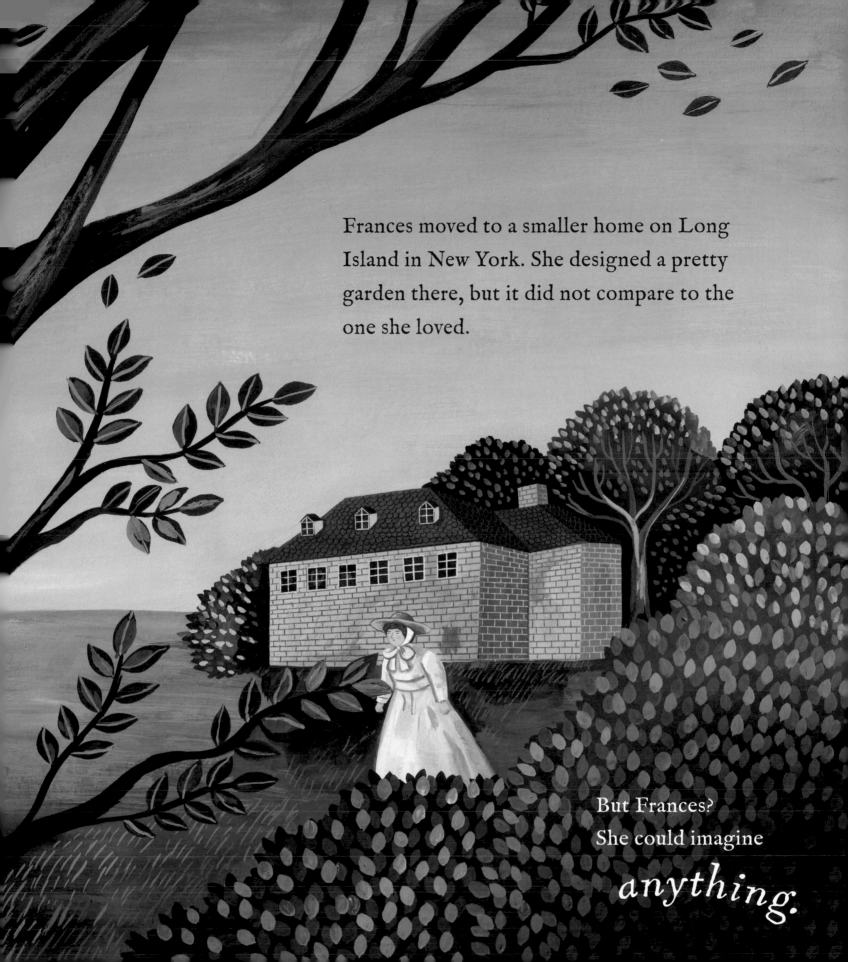

Frances moved to a smaller home on Long Island in New York. She designed a pretty garden there, but it did not compare to the one she loved.

But Frances?
She could imagine

anything.

Putting pen to paper, she dreamed up the most *beautiful* garden in the world. Her robin was there. Her roses, too, and the locked door from the city, and the trees and lilacs she had loved as a girl. So was a dear boy who healed as Lionel never could.

The Secret Garden

Frances *poured* her love and grief and memory into the imaginary garden, and the book—for it was a book—was published a short while later. The garden—*The Secret Garden*—became as real to millions of readers as it was to her, a place where *hope* is never far for those who can imagine . . .

anything.

**1849 — 1924**

# More About Frances Hodgson Burnett

Frances Hodgson Burnett lived a rags-to-riches life, like the characters in many of her books. From humble beginnings in England, she moved to America and later became the highest-earning woman in the United States.

As a child, Frances attended "dame schools" in houses near hers, dropping out before high school. A voracious reader, she regretted her lack of education and, after being published, gratefully accepted a reading list her editor offered so she could continue her education.

She began writing as a child—romantic adventure stories about long-haired heroines, evil villains, and handsome noblemen. In her teens she wrote more realistic stories focused on character in addition to plot. Until she was published, she was so poor that finding paper to write on was always a struggle.

Most of her fifty-two books were serious novels for adults. Many addressed the relationship between Americans and the British. Often she wrote in dialect, which came easily to her when speaking or writing.

Her first book for children, *Little Lord Fauntleroy* (1886), was the *Harry Potter* of its day. It sold hundreds of thousands of copies and was translated into dozens of languages. Stores sold clothing and souvenirs based on the novel. The book, illustrated by Reginald Birch, popularized a style of dressing that little boys, like Frances's sons, hated: long hair, velvet suits, and lace collars. She had to tell her boys "Hair Curling Stories" to hold them still while combing their hair into ringlets.

Financial success allowed Frances to divide her time between England and the United States. She crossed the Atlantic thirty-three times. By Victorian standards, her life was shocking: she smoked cigarettes, spent time away from her children, divorced her first husband, and then married a man ten years her junior; that marriage lasted two years.

Frances lived luxuriously, enjoying the company of famous friends like Louisa May Alcott, Mary Mapes Dodge, Henry James, Ellen Terry, Mark Twain, Oscar Wilde, and Israel Zangwill. After leaving Maytham, she had a house built on Long Island. Her son Vivian lived nearby with his wife and two daughters. In 1905 Frances became a United States citizen; later she campaigned in New York for women's suffrage.

When movies grew popular, Frances thought them less wholesome than theater. She changed her mind on a 1913 trip to Austria, where she saw a crowd enjoying a silent film, even though the captions were in English. Convinced that movies could communicate across cultures, she saw several of her books made into silent films. She attended the New York premiere of the 1921 movie *Little Lord Fauntleroy*, in which, thanks to special effects, actress Mary Pickford played both Fauntleroy and his mother.

Frances died of colon cancer at her home in Plandome, New York, on October 29, 1924. In 1937, a statue by sculptor Bessie Potter Vonnoh was dedicated to her in Central Park in New York, where it still stands. It portrays two figures: Dickon and Mary from *The Secret Garden*.

After Frances's death, *Little Lord Fauntleroy*'s fame faded, but two of her other children's titles remain popular: *A Little Princess* (1905) and *The Secret Garden* (1911), now her most famous book. Though not especially popular in her lifetime, *The Secret Garden* was aways a favorite with readers. By the end of the 1970s, thanks to growing academic interest in children's literature and numerous newly illustrated editions of the book, it was considered a classic. Many scholars have called it "the most significant children's book of the twentieth century."

In 1911, *The Secret Garden* was considered modern and healthful for emphasizing positive thinking and the connection between childhood and nature. In recent years, *A Little Princess* and *The Secret Garden* have faced criticism for Frances's colonialist treatment of people from India. Her defenders say that the kindest characters in *A Little Princess* are an Indian servant and the British man he works for. They say *The Secret Garden* sends the message that colonialism harms souls, making the white people who benefitted from it arrogant and unkind. However these books are regarded, they reflect attitudes in British society that predominated in the early 1900s. Today parents or teachers can discuss with young readers the contrast between these ideas and how our culture has changed.

New versions of Frances's books continue to appear as movies, television programs, and plays. An internationally successful musical, *The Secret Garden*, opened on Broadway in 1991. Some new treatments make direct efforts to correct Frances's

prejudices. Amir Wilson, a British-Sudanese actor, played Dickon in the 2020 film *The Secret Garden*. The musical has been updated, using Hindi words and music and casting Indian actors in the early scenes. New book versions, including graphic novels, make Frances's characters more diverse—Asian, or brown-skinned, or even homosexual, and thus still controversial. Her books remain beloved by many generations of readers.

## TIMELINE

- **1849:** November 24. Frances "Fanny" Eliza Hodgson is born in Manchester, England.
- **1853:** Her father dies of a stroke; her mother takes over the family store.
- **1855:** The family moves from the country to Manchester.
- **1861:** The Civil War in the American South cuts off cotton supplies to Manchester factories.
- **1862:** Manchester businesses fail.
- **1863:** Frances's mother sells the family store.
- **1865:** Frances moves with her family to New Market, Tennessee, at the end of the Civil War.
- **1868:** Frances's first published story appears in *Godey's Lady's Book*.
- **1869:** Frances moves her mother and sisters to Knoxville.
- **1872:** Frances returns to England for a visit.
- **1873:** Frances marries Swan Burnett in Tennessee.
- **1874:** Frances gives birth to son Lionel in Tennessee.
- **1875:** The Burnetts move to Paris.
- **1876:** Frances gives birth to son Vivian in Paris.
- **1877:** The Burnetts move to Washington, DC
- **1887:** Frances takes Lionel and Vivian to London, Paris, and Italy.
- **1888:** Frances wins a copyright lawsuit against a writer who adapted *Little Lord Fauntleroy* into a play.
- **1888:** Frances opens her own *Little Lord Fauntleroy* play, a smash hit on both sides of the Atlantic.
- **1890:** Lionel dies in Paris.
- **1890:** Lionel's doctor, Stephen Townesend, becomes Frances's business manager.
- **1898:** Frances divorces Swan Burnett.
- **1898:** Frances leases Maytham Hall in Kent and restores its walled garden.
- **1898:** Vivian graduates from Harvard.
- **1900:** Frances marries Stephen Townesend in Italy.

- *1902:* Frances tells Stephen Townesend their marriage is over.

- *1907:* Frances must leave Maytham Hall when the owner wants to sell.

- *1908:* Frances builds a house on Long Island and invites her sister Edith to live with her.

- *1911:* Frances and Edith spend winters in Bermuda.

- *1913:* Frances sees Austrians enjoying American silent movies.

- *1914:* World War I breaks out in Europe.

- *1914:* Vivian, a writer and editor, marries Constance Buel; they have two daughters.

- *1918:* World War I ends.

- *1921:* Frances attends the opening of the Hollywood movie *Little Lord Fauntleroy.*

- *1924:* October 29. Frances dies at Plandome.

## SELECTED FRANCES HODGSON BURNETT BOOKS FOR CHILDREN

- *Little Lord Fauntleroy.* 1886. Inheriting a title, an American boy goes to live with his grumpy grandfather in England, where he wins the old man over with his democratic ways.

- *Editha's Burglar.* 1888. When seven-year-old Editha encounters a burglar in her house, she asks him to be quiet so he won't scare her mother.

- *Sara Crewe, or What Happened at Miss Minchin's.* 1888. A rich girl's father brings her from India to a British boarding school. When he dies, she becomes a servant in the school.

- *A Little Princess.* 1905. Burnett rewrote her short book, *Sara Crewe,* as a popular play and renamed it *A Little Princess* (she made as much money from her plays as she did from her books). Later she expanded the play into this longer novel.

- *Racketty-Packetty House.* 1906. A story of two dollhouses, one old and shabby, one new and grand. The shabby dolls have more fun than the fancy ones.

- *The Secret Garden.* 1911. Mary Lennox, a troubled orphan, comes from India to live with her uncle in Yorkshire, England. Mary and her unhappy, bedridden cousin, Colin, heal themselves by caring for a neglected, walled garden. They are helped by Dickon, a neighbor boy, and a friendly robin. The book is unusual because its heroine is so disagreeable. Young readers love the idea of a secret known only to the children.

- *The Lost Prince.* 1915. Two boys, one a street urchin, the other, the son of a prince, help restore the prince to his rightful position as ruler of Samavia.

## Selected Frances Hodgson Burnett Books for Adults

- *That Lass o' Lowrie's.* 1877. Frances's first novel features a "pit girl" who works in the Lancashire coal mines. She stands up to her abusive father and befriends an unwed mother.

- *Surly Tim.* 1877. A tragedy in which a weaver caught and crushed by a loom tells his own story in Lancashire dialect.

- *Dolly.* 1877. Although set in London, this novel reflects Frances's "Bohemian" life in Knoxville. Freedom and unconventionality compensate a poor family for a lack of money.

- *Haworth's.* 1879. In Lancashire, a runaway boy collapses in the snow in front of an iron foundry. Later a young American comes to the industrial area his father left decades before.

- *Louisiana.* 1880. Novella. A New York girl, on holiday in North Carolina, decides to remake a simple farmer's daughter in her own image. This gentle satire defends simple values.

- *A Fair Barbarian.* 1881. A wealthy American girl, wearing diamonds in the daytime, shakes up the English village of Slowbridge when she comes to visit her aunt.

- *Through One Administration.* 1883. In Washington, DC, an unhappy marriage endures through a presidential administration. The heroine longs to live a freer life, like men.

- *The One I Knew the Best of All.* 1893. An autobiography of Frances's childhood and her move from England to America. Illustrated by Reginald Birch, who also did pictures for *Little Lord Fauntleroy*.

- *A Lady of Quality.* 1896. Clorinda, a foul-mouthed girl raised as a boy, accidentally kills her lover and hides the body in the basement of her London townhouse. Later she finds love.

- *The Making of a Marchioness.* 1901. Spinster Emily Fox-Seton, poor but well-born, is invited to help with (meaning "work at") a house party at a stately home, and the wealthy owner falls in love with her.

- *The Dawn of a To-Morrow.* 1906. Novella. A wealthy man, suffering from an unnamed illness, is saved from suicide by an uneducated London street girl.

- *The Shuttle.* 1907. A cruel, impoverished British nobleman marries a wealthy American girl and separates her from her family. The setting for this book is based on Maytham Hall.

## Bibliography

Burnett, Constance Buel. *Happily Ever After: A Portrait of Frances Hodgson Burnett*. New York: Vanguard, 1965. A biography for children by Frances's daughter-in-law.

Burnett, Frances Hodgson. *The Annotated Secret Garden*. Edited with an Introduction and Notes by Gretchen Holbrook Gerzina. New York: Norton, 2007.

Burnett, Vivian. *The Romantick Lady (Frances Hodgson Burnett): The Life Story of an Imagination*. New York: Scribner, 1927. A biography by Frances's son.

Carpenter, Angelica Shirley, and Jean Shirley. *Frances Hodgson Burnett: Beyond the Secret Garden*. Minneapolis: Lerner, 1990. A biography for young people.

Carpenter, Angelica Shirley, ed. *In the Garden: Essays in Honor of Frances Hodgson Burnett*. Lanham, Maryland: Scarecrow Press, 2006.

Gerzina, Gretchen Holbrook. *Frances Hodgson Burnett: The Unexpected Life of the Author of* The Secret Garden. Rutgers University Press, 2004.

McDowell, Marta. *Unearthing The Secret Garden: The Plants & Places That Inspired Frances Hodgson Burnett*. Portland, Oregon: Timber Press, 2021.

Riazi, Karuna. *A Bit of Earth*. Greenwillow Books, 2023. This modern retelling of *The Secret Garden* features a Pakistani-Bangladeshi Muslim heroine who moves to Long Island. However, the book doesn't mention the original author's name.

Streatfeild, Noel. *Movie Shoes*. New York: Dell Publishing, 1984, 1949. Published in Great Britain as *The Painted Garden*, Collins, 2000, 1949. An English girl, vacationing in California with her family, gets a starring role as Mary in a Hollywood movie of *The Secret Garden*.

Thwaite, Ann. *Beyond the Secret Garden: The Life of Frances Hodgson Burnett*. London: Duckworth, 2020. Audio Book, Tantor Media, 2023.

———. *Waiting for the Party: The Life of Frances Hodgson Burnett*, London: Secker & Warburg, 1974; republished as Beyond the Secret Garden: The Life of Frances Hodgson Burnett, London: Duckworth, 2020. Audio book, Tantor Media, 2023.

Weir, Ivy Noelle. *The Secret Garden on 81st Street: A Modern Graphic Retelling of The Secret Garden*. Illustrated by Amber Padilla. New York: Little, Brown and Company, 2021.

# How to Cultivate Your Imagination, Now and When You Grow Up

## *A Letter from Fanny's Family*

Dear Young Reader,

Did you know that my great-great-grandmother Frances was almost sixty years old when she dreamt up and began writing *The Secret Garden*? That's pretty old! And sometimes, when grown-ups grow up, they forget how to use their imagination—but not Frances. She could imagine anything, like a vision of a locked-away garden being found and brought back to life with magic, or a taskmaster fairy she named Queen Crosspatch, who sat on her shoulder and whispered the words for the books *Racketty-Packetty House* and *Queen Silver Bell* so Frances could obediently write them down.

She made it a practice to use her active imagination throughout her life to

- turn weeds into wildflowers
- make hard things, like moving, an adventure
- change her dreary surroundings from gray to green
- face challenges and changes
- throw parties and spread joy
- empathize with the poor near her homes
- make friends with a robin
- deal with sad things and celebrate glad things
- break down walls and open doors for other women to walk through
- plan her spring gardens in the dead of winter.

Are you good at using your imagination, too? I'll bet you are!

In my job, as the family keeper of all things Frances, I get a chance to exercise my imagination often when I go digging through her more than fifty books to find the keys and messages of hope that I believe she intentionally left behind to inspire and encourage us today.

And guess what! I recently discovered that Frances tucked some extra-special keys into the pages of *The Secret Garden* that can help us to cultivate the seeds of our imaginations for years to come. I've put nine of them in this book, so keep reading! And keep on imagining, my friend, and never lose hope!

Blessings and blooms,

Keri Wilt
*Great-great-granddaughter of Frances Hodgson Burnett, speaker, writer, podcast host, and life-gardener, who is on a mission to plant seeds of hope via www.TheWell-TendedLife.com*

### Key #1: Daydream

Daydreaming can unlock your imagination! Simply sit still and let your mind and thoughts float like a "little snow-white cloud" in a positive direction. Set a timer for 10 minutes and give it a try.

*"The high, deep, blue sky arched over Misselthwaite as well as over the moor, and she kept lifting her face and looking up into it, trying to imagine what it would be like to lie down on one of the little snow-white clouds and float about."*

### Key #2: Wonder

Wondering can jumpstart creativity and help your brain see things that do not yet exist. So, wonder about something today with your family at the dinner table or in the car. Ask open-ended questions like, If flowers could sing, what would they sound like? And remember, don't use Google . . . use your imagination!

*"She could not help thinking about the garden which no one had been into for ten years. She wondered what it would look like and whether there were any flowers still alive in it."*

### Key #3 Play

Play is not just good for your body—it's a great way to warm up, stretch, and strengthen your imagination muscles, too! So, make time to purposely play each day for at least 30 minutes.

*"Let her play out in th' fresh air skippin' an' it'll stretch her legs an' arms an' give her some strength in 'em."*

### Key #4 Read

Some books contain a good kind of magic that can open your mind! Ask your local librarian for some suggestions and make reading a regular part of each day. Then work your imagination by dreaming up a new ending to the story.

*"The Magic works best when you work yourself," he said this morning. "You can feel it in your bones and muscles. I am going to read books about bones and muscles, but I am going to write a book about Magic. I am making it up now. I keep finding out things."*

### Key #5 Wander

A brisk walk, on or off a path, can help clear the way for your imagination to run wild. It sounds silly, but when training your mind to wander, it sometimes helps to make your body do it first. Talk with your parents about where you can safely wander, and then give this key to cultivating your imagination a try.

*"She walked round and round the gardens and wandered about the paths in the park."*

### Key #6 Think

Your thoughts and imagination are as powerful as electric batteries! One way you can keep them charged up is by starting a gratitude/joy journal. Take a few minutes each day to write down three things you are grateful for or that brought you joy, and you'll begin to notice more sunlight streaming into your mind.

*"One of the new things people began to find out in the last century was that thoughts—just mere thoughts—are as powerful as electric batteries—as good for one as sunlight is, or as bad for one as poison."*

### KEY #7 STOP AND TRY

When you get older, you tend to get busier . . . which leaves little room for your imagination to bloom. So make it a habit now to slow down long enough to imagine what your life will look like when it is in full bloom.

*"Sometimes she stopped digging to look at the garden and try to imagine what it would be like when it was covered with thousands of lovely things in bloom."*

### KEY #8 VISUALIZE

Did you know that this two-word phrase, "even if," can help us see through the storms to the rainbows and sunshine? Use these two words, along with your imagination, the next time you are going through a hard time to visualize the good that lies ahead when the clouds finally part.

*"Even if the roses are dead, there are other things alive."*

### KEY #9: BELIEVE

Did you know that most new ideas seem a bit strange at first? Just imagine what people said when they heard for the first time about electricity, telephones, or computers! A big part of cultivating an active imagination is learning to suspend our disbelief just long enough until hope can take hold. Give it a try!

*"At first people refuse to believe that a strange new thing can be done, then they begin to hope it can be done, then they see it can be done—then it is done and all the world wonders why it was not done centuries ago."*

## About the Author

Angelica Shirley Carpenter writes biographies for young people and older readers, too. Her subjects are authors, including Frances Hodgson Burnett, L. Frank Baum, Robert Louis Stevenson, Lewis Carroll, and others. She lives with her husband in Fresno, California. A self-proclaimed Oz nut, she is a past president of the International Wizard of Oz Club. In her former life she was a librarian, the founding curator of the Arne Nixon Center for the Study of Children's Literature at California State University, Fresno.

## About the Illustrator

Helena Pérez García is a Spanish illustrator whose work has appeared across magazines, newspapers, packaging, and books for children and adults internationally. Helena's primary medium is gouache, and her main sources of inspiration are art, literature, and cinema. Some of her clients include Penguin Random House, The Body Shop, Tate Publishing, *The Financial Times*, *Reader's Digest*, and *Il Corriere della Sera*, amongst many others.